RU

D0997580

700003092171X

The Ultimate Guide to Rugby

Gavin Mortimer

This book was conceived, edited and designed for Puffin Books by
Tony Potter Publishing Ltd
tonypotter.com
Illustrators: John Cooper & Brett Hudson
Layouts: Sue Rose

WORCESTERSHIRE COUNTY COUNCIL	
171	
Bertrams	25.08.07
J796.333	£5.99
RU	

PUFFIN BOOKS

Published by the Penguin Group

Penguin Books Ltd, 80 Strand, London WC2R ORL, England

Penguin Group (USA) Inc., 375 Hudson Street, New York, New York 10014, USA

Penguin Group (Canada), 90 Eglinton Avenue East, Suite 700, Toronto, Ontario, Canada M4P 2Y3

(a division of Pearson Penguin Canada Inc.)

Penguin Ireland, 25 St Stephen's Green, Dublin 2, Ireland (a division of Penguin Books Ltd)

Penguin Group (Australia), 250 Camberwell Road, Camberwell, Victoria 3124, Australia

(a division of Pearson Australia Group Pty Ltd)

Penguin Books India Pvt Ltd, 11 Community Centre, Panchsheel Park, New Delhi – 110 017, India

Penguin Group (NZ), 67 Apollo Drive, Rosedale, North Shore 0632, New Zealand

(a division of Pearson New Zealand Ltd)

Penguin Books (South Africa) (Pty) Ltd, 24 Sturdee Avenue, Rosebank, Johannesburg 2196, South Africa

Penguin Books Ltd, Registered Offices: 80 Strand, London WC2R 0RL, England

puffinbooks.com

First published 2007

1

Text copyright © Tony Potter Publishing Ltd, 2007

Illustrations copyright © Tony Potter Publishing / Getty Images Ltd, 2007

All rights reserved

The moral right of the author and illustrators has been asserted

Made and printed in Dubai

Except in the United States of America, this book is sold subject to the conditions that it shall not, by way of trade or otherwise, be lent, re-sold, hired out, or otherwise circulated without the publisher's prior consent in any form of binding or cover other than that in which it is published and without a similar condition including this condition being imposed on the subsequent purchaser

British Library Cataloguing in Publication Data

A CIP catalogue record for this book is available from the British Library

ISBN: 978-0-141-32321-3

Contents

We Have Lift Off

South Africa's Hilton Lobberts hitches a lift on the back of England prop Phil Vickery during a 2006 match at Twickenham

The Dream Team

NO. 15

Josh Lewsey
(England)

Full name: Joshua Owen Lewsey

Position: Full-back

Born: 30 November 1976 in Bromley, Kent

Height: 180cm

Weight: 87kg

Club: London Wasps

Test debut: 1998 vs New Zealand

Honours: 46 England caps and 3 Lions caps

Magic moment: Winning the 2003 World Cup

Did you know? Josh used to be in the army

What other position has Josh played for England?

5

The World is Oval

Canada: Rugby was first played in Canada in the 1860s and the union was formed in 1929. Canada have played in every World Cup and made the quarter-finals in 1991.

Ireland: Ireland began playing rugby in the 1850s – although a similar game called 'Caid' had been popular for centuries. Ireland's first match was against England in 1875.

Scotland: Scotland beat England in the first ever international match and in 1873 the Scottish Rugby Union was formed. Rugby is most popular in Edinburgh.

Wales: Rugby came to Wales in 1850 thanks to schoolmaster Rowland Williams who brought it over from England, and Wales' first match was in 1881 against England.

USA: A form of rugby was played at American universities in the 1860s and at the 1924 Olympics the USA beat France to win the gold medal at rugby.

England: The birthplace of the sport in 1823 at Rugby School and it was England who played Scotland in the first ever international match in 1871.

France: The first French club was formed in 1872, although they didn't play their first Test match until 1906. Rugby is played more in the south of France than the north.

Uruguay: Their first rugby international was in 1948 against Chile and Uruguay are now the second strongest country in South America after Argentina.

Argentina: Rugby first appeared in Argentina in the 1880s thanks to British immigrants and Argentina reached the World Cup quarter-final in 1999.

Spain: Rugby was first played in the north of Spain 100 years ago, thanks to French workers who took the sport across the border. Spain played in the 1999 World Cup.

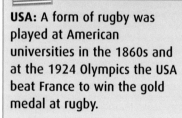

Romania: Romanian students returning from France brought rugby with them 100 years ago and in 1919 they played their first ever match against the USA.

Japan: British sailors introduced rugby in the 1870s and it soon became popular in universities. In 1929 the union was formed and an Australian side toured Japan in 1934.

Samoa: Samoa played their first ever match in 1924 against Fiji but didn't begin playing regular international matches until the 1970s when the team toured New Zealand.

Georgia: Rugby has been played in Georgia for 80 years but their first international match was against Zimbabwe in 1989, and since then the game has gained popularity there.

Fiji: British soldiers introduced rugby in the 1880s and in 1924 Fiji played their first Test match, although since then they have become better known in Sevens.

Italy: Rugby in Italy is most popular in the north, where it was first played in the 1920s by workers returning from France. In 2000 Italy joined the Six Nations.

Australia: Australia was the first country outside Britain to take up rugby, when it was introduced in 1864 and they are the only nation to have won the World Cup twice.

South Africa: British soldiers introduced rugby in the 1870s when they were serving in South Africa and in 1891 a British side toured the country and played 19 matches.

Namibia: Namibia became a country when it gained independence from South Africa in 1990 and in 1999 they played in their first World Cup.

Tonga: Missionaries established rugby in the small Pacific Island in the early 20th Century and in 1924 Tonga beat Fiji 9-6 in their first ever international.

New Zealand: A former English schoolboy called Charles Monro brought rugby to the country in 1870, and in 1884 a New Zealand team toured Australia.

The Dream Team

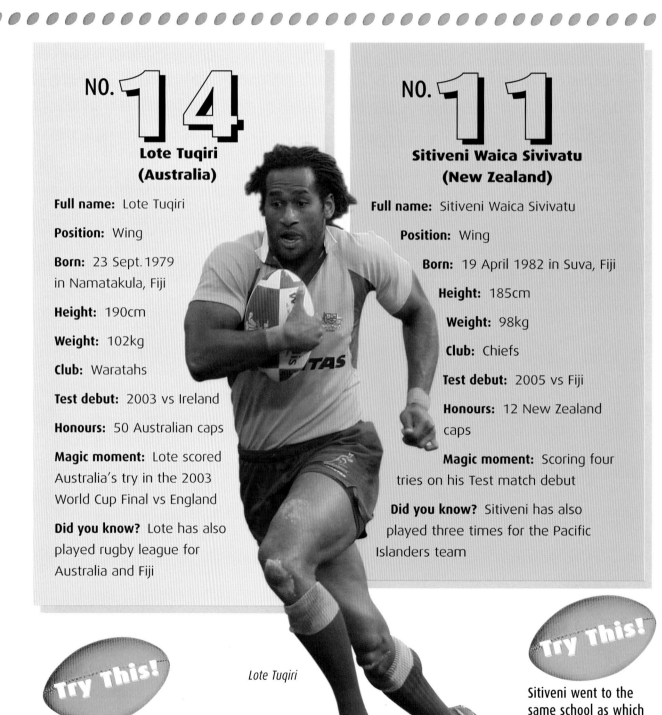

NO. 14

Lote Tuqiri
(Australia)

Full name: Lote Tuqiri

Position: Wing

Born: 23 Sept. 1979 in Namatakula, Fiji

Height: 190cm

Weight: 102kg

Club: Waratahs

Test debut: 2003 vs Ireland

Honours: 50 Australian caps

Magic moment: Lote scored Australia's try in the 2003 World Cup Final vs England

Did you know? Lote has also played rugby league for Australia and Fiji

NO. 11

Sitiveni Waica Sivivatu
(New Zealand)

Full name: Sitiveni Waica Sivivatu

Position: Wing

Born: 19 April 1982 in Suva, Fiji

Height: 185cm

Weight: 98kg

Club: Chiefs

Test debut: 2005 vs Fiji

Honours: 12 New Zealand caps

Magic moment: Scoring four tries on his Test match debut

Did you know? Sitiveni has also played three times for the Pacific Islanders team

Lote Tuqiri

Try This!

Which other position has Lote played for Australia?

Try This!

Sitiveni went to the same school as which other whale-sized New Zealand wing?

8

Sidestep Back in Time

A rugby timeline from 1823 to 2006, detailing the evolution of the game.

The Webb Ellis trophy at the graveside of William Webb Ellis

1823: William Webb Ellis, a pupil at England's Rugby school, catches the ball and runs with it during a game of football.

1858: The world's first rugby club is founded at Blackheath in London.

1871: The Rugby Football Union is formed by 20 English clubs and in the same year England and Scotland contest the first rugby international.

1886: The International Rugby Board is formed.

1897: Jerseys become numbered.

1910: England play their first match at Twickenham.

1931: France are thrown out of the Five Nations for paying their players and don't return until 1946.

1968: Replacements allowed for injured players.

1987: New Zealand win the first World Cup by beating France.

1993: England win the first World Cup Sevens.

1995: South Africa win the World Cup and a few weeks later rugby becomes professional.

1996: South Africa, Australia and New Zealand contest the first Tri-Nations.

1996: Substitutes are allowed.

2000: Italy join the Five Nations to make it Six.

2003: England are the first Northern Hemisphere side to win the World Cup.

Francois Pienaar accepts the 1995 World Cup from Nelson Mandela

Ruck and Roll

Do you know your garryowen from your grubber? Get to grips with rugby's funny phrases.

Against the head: If the opposition wins the ball at your scrum.

Breakdown: Where the play stops (breaks down) on the field after the ball-carrier is tackled.

Crooked feed: If the scrum-half puts ('feeds') the ball into the scrum at an angle instead of straight down the middle. A free-kick offence.

Crossing: If a player without the ball runs in front of a team-mate with the ball, thus obstructing the opposition tacklers.

Dummy: When you trick an opponent by pretending to pass the ball to one of your team-mates.

Free kick: Awarded for technical offences such as a crooked feed (see above). A team cannot kick for points from a free kick.

Gain line: An imaginary line on the pitch that the ball-carrying team advance across from a scrum or ruck to gain territory.

Garryowen: An attacking kick that goes up high and comes down in the opposition territory (also called an Up and Under).

Grubber: An attacking kick that bounces along the ground.

Hand off: When the ball-carrier pushes away a tackler with the open palm of his hand.

Hospital pass: A poor pass to a team-mate meaning he has to catch the ball at the moment he is tackled.

Killing the ball: When a player on the defending side illegally dives on the ball to prevent the attacking team gaining quick possession.

Knock on: When a player knocks the ball forward with his hands as he tries to catch it.

Line-out: Means of restarting play when the ball goes into touch.

Mark: When a player catches the ball behind his 22-metre line and shouts 'mark', play stops and he is allowed to kick the ball away.

Maul: When the ball-carrier is held by opposing players and his team-mates then bind on to him to try to keep the ball.

Not straight: What the referee calls if the ball isn't thrown into a line-out exactly down the middle of the two lines of forwards. A free kick is awarded to the other side.

Overlap: When the ball is passed along the line of backs and the attacking team has more runners than the defending team has tacklers.

Penalty: Awarded for a range of offences and for which a team can, if they choose, try to score points by kicking the ball through the posts.

Pushover try: When the attacking team at a scrum pushes back the opposition over the try-line and touches down the ball for a try.

Recycle: When the attacking team regains possession of the ball at a ruck or tackle.

Rolling maul: When the team in possession of the ball move the maul towards the opposition try-line.

Ruck: Where one or more players from each team contest the ball on the ground while staying on their feet.

Scissors: When the ball-carrier passes the ball to a team-mate running forward in the opposite direction.

Scrum: Means of restarting the game after, for example, a forward pass or a knock on, with the two sets of forwards engaging one another.

If a player is sent to the sin bin, what colour card is he shown by the referee?

Sidestep: A means of avoiding a tackler by pretending to move one way, but then moving the other.

Sin bin: If a player commits a deliberate offence or is guilty of foul play he can be sent off the pitch, to the sin bin, for ten minutes.

Spear tackle: An illegal tackle that involves picking up the ball-carrier and throwing him to the ground head-first.

Turnover ball: When the defending team gains possession of the ball at a ruck or tackle.

King of the Kickers

They're the players who put the boot into the opposition – the kickers with a cool head and a fab foot!

Rugby is a team game, of course, with all 15 players working together to win the match, but it's the goalkickers who are often the difference between a victory and a defeat.

Look at **Jonny Wilkinson** in the 2003 World Cup! He helped England win the trophy with the awesome accuracy of his kicking in every game of the tournament. And what about Ireland when they lifted the 2006 Triple Crown? **Ronan O'Gara** didn't miss many kicks.

Yes, behind every team there is a great goalkicker, slotting penalties, knocking over conversions and sometimes dropping goals like the wonderful Wilkinson!

Who is your country's king of the kickers? Is it Ronan O'Gara of Ireland, Australia's super **Stephen Larkham** or the ace All Black **Dan Carter**?

Look at how Ronan O'Gara keeps his eye on the ball as he kicks

Penalties are usually what win rugby matches. Tries are terrific but they're harder to score than penalties.

Penalties are awarded when the opposition break the rules. Sometimes they're 40 metres from the posts, other times they are bang in front. But follow our instructions and it won't matter from where you kick your penalty – it will sail between the posts for three points and a big pat on the back from your teammates!

1 Place the ball on a tee or a small mound of mud so it is upright or leaning slightly forward. You want to be able to see the ball's 'sweet spot', which is about one-third of the way up the ball.

2 Measure a run-up that feels comfortable for you and then approach the ball in a curved run with your eyes looking at the ball and not at the goalposts.

3 As you reach the ball your non-kicking foot should be as close to it as possible, your body weight slightly forward and your eyes still concentrating on the 'sweet spot'.

4 It should be the instep of your boot that makes contact with the ball and your foot must follow through with the toes pointing in the direction of the ball. Only take your eyes off the ball after you've followed through – and let's hope you'll see it soaring between the goalposts!

The Dream Team

NO. 13

Brian O'Driscoll
(Ireland)

Full name: Brian Gerald O'Driscoll

Position: Centre

Born: 21 January 1979 in Dublin, Ireland

Height: 178cm

Weight: 95kg

Club: Leinster

Test debut: 1999 vs Australia

Honours: 72 Ireland caps and 4 Lions caps

Magic moment: Captaining Ireland to the Triple Crown in 2004 and 2006

Did you know? Brian captained the Lions against New Zealand in 2005

NO. 12

Gavin Henson
(Wales)

Full name: Gavin Lloyd Henson

Position: Centre

Born: 1 February 1982 in Bridgend, Wales

Height: 183cm

Weight: 98kg

Club: The Ospreys

Test debut: 2001 vs Japan

Honours: 20 Wales caps and 1 Lions cap

Magic moment: Kicking the winning penalty vs England in 2005

Did you know? Gavin will soon appear in a film with Hollywood superstar Catherine Zeta-Jones about a small rugby team in Wales who get a new coach

Ireland's Brian O'Driscoll is a centre of excellence

Try This! Why is Brian's nickname BOD?

Try This! Who is Gavin's famous singing girlfriend?

Terrific Pacific

Their countries are small but, boy, their players aren't!

Tonga, Fiji and Samoa…do you know where they are? Look at an atlas and you'll find these islands in the Pacific Ocean, north of New Zealand. Aren't they tiny? But ask anyone who's ever played against a frightening Fijian, a terrifying Tongan or a scary Samoan, and they'll tell you there's certainly nothing small about their rugby players!

Since rugby was introduced to the Pacific Islanders over 100 years ago, they have earned a reputation as some of the world's most talented players. Why? Well, they're big and strong, fast and athletic. In fact, they have everything – even a war dance that they perform before each international match, just like the All Blacks' Haka!

The Fijians call their dance the 'Cibi', the Samoans have the 'Siva Tau' and the Tongans' war dance is known as the 'Kailao'.

Unfortunately, a lot of players from these Pacific Islands end up playing for New Zealand and Australia because their families have to move to these bigger countries to find better jobs.

Did you know, for example, that the most famous rugby player ever – Jonah Lomu of New Zealand – has Tongan parents? Or that Australian wing Lote Tuqiri was born in Fiji, or that All Black No 8 Rodney So'oialo comes from Samoa?

Although Tonga, Fiji and Samoa play in the World Cup as individual countries, the three Islands also play together in a team called the Pacific Islanders. In 2006 they toured Britain and wowed everyone with their brilliant brand of rugby.

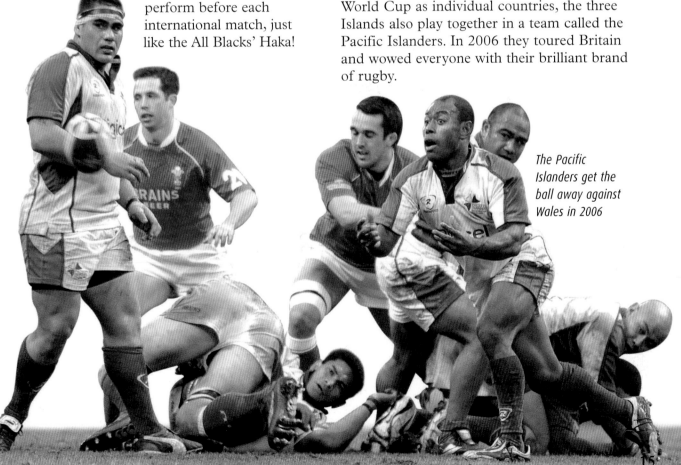

The Pacific Islanders get the ball away against Wales in 2006

15

Respect the Ref

Rugby has a great tradition for respecting the referee. Unlike football, where players shout at the referee, rugby players aren't even allowed to talk to the ref. If they do, they'll be penalised, or even sent to the sin bin to cool down for ten minutes!

The only people who can talk to the referee on a rugby pitch are the two captains, and even then they must be polite and show good manners!

The referee is always assisted by two touch judges, and if they see some dirty play or spot a forward pass, they're allowed to point it out to the referee. That's why when you watch a rugby match on TV, you can see little microphones attached to the shirts of the touch judges and the referees – so they can talk to one another!

For a lot of important matches, like the Six Nations and the World Cup, there is also a video referee. He sits in the stadium in front of a TV and video. If the referee can't decide whether a try has been scored because the ball is under a pile of bodies, he can ask the video ref to watch a slow-motion reply of the incident. Then it's up to the video ref to say if a try was scored or not – let's hope he hasn't nipped out for a tea break!

During a match a rugby ref makes a lot of signals so that the players know what his decisions are. But if you didn't know anything about rugby you might think the ref was doing some keep fit exercises! Opposite are six of the most common signals. Why not practise them yourself, and pretty soon you'll be a rugby ref with lots of respect!

Try awarded

The referee indicates that a team has scored a try.

Penalty awarded

The referee indicates that a team has committed an offence for which he has awarded a penalty.

Scrum awarded

The referee indicates that play will be restarted with a scrum.

Ball knocked on

The referee indicates that a player has knocked the ball forward for which there will be a scrum.

Advantage being played

The referee indicates that a team has conceded a penalty but he is allowing play to continue for a while.

Forward pass

The referee indicates that the ball was passed forward instead of backwards which means there will be a scrum.

Six of the Best

First it was four, then it was five, now it is Six Nations, but one thing never changes - rugby's oldest international tournament is full of fabulous action!

Wales celebrate winning the Grand Slam in 2005

Although England played Scotland way back in 1871, it wasn't until 1883 that England, Scotland, Wales and Ireland (who call themselves the 'Home Nations') played each other every year in a competition that at first was called the International Championship.

In 1910 France joined the tournament and the Five Nations championship was born. The next year Wales won all four of its matches – a brilliant feat that came to be called a 'Grand Slam'. The expression is still used today to describe the team that not only

wins the Six Nations title but also wins all its matches. But it's not easy to do. Since 1910 the Grand Slam has been won only 33 times!

England have won the most 'Slams' with 12, then Wales (nine), France (eight) Scotland (three) and Ireland (one). Italy have never won the Grand Slam, but give them time!

Italy only entered the Six Nations in 2000 and it will be a few more years before they are as good as the other five countries. Look at France. Although they joined the competition in 1910 it wasn't

until 1959 that they finished first in the Five Nations.

But one thing that Italy will never be able to win is the Triple Crown, and neither will France! The Triple Crown is awarded to the country when one of the Home Nations beats each of the other three. Why is it called the Triple Crown? Hundreds of years ago there was a King called James I, who was the first king to rule the triple kingdoms of Scotland, Ireland and England. (Wales was part of England then.) So people said he had a 'triple crown'!

Six Nations Stats

Grand Slams are hard to come by, but did you know that four players have won four of them! The first was Englishman Cyril Lowe, who achieved the amazing feat in 1913 and 1914, and again in 1921 and 1923. Another Englishman, Jason Leonard, won his in 1991, '92, '95 and 2003, and two Frenchmen, Olivier Magne and Fabien Pelous took the honours in 1997, 1998, 2002 and 2004. What a fantastic four!

England won the very first International Championship in 1883; the first title when it became the Five Nations in 1910; and the first title when it became the Six Nations in 2000.

Wales were wonderful in the 1970s, winning the Grand Slam in 1971, '76 and '78. Although they didn't snap up a 'Slam' in the 1980s and 1990s, they roared to a glorious Grand Slam success in 2005 – their first for 27 years!

Ireland's only Grand Slam was in 1948 but they have won the Triple Crown eight times, including 2004 and 2006.

Scotland have won the Triple Crown ten times, including 1938, when not only did they beat England at Twickenham, but the match was televised – the first time a Five Nations was shown on the TV!

Italy's first ever match in the Six Nations was in Rome against Scotland in 2000. Everyone thought the Scots would win easily, but Italy pulled off a shock 34-20 win.

France and Wales contest the ball in a 1931 Five Nations match

19

The Dream Team

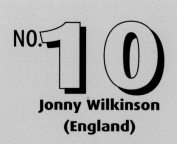

NO. 10
Jonny Wilkinson
(England)

Full name: Jonny Peter Wilkinson

Position: Fly-half

Born: 25 May 1979 in Frimley, Surrey

Height: 178cm

Weight: 85kg

Club: Newcastle Falcons

Test debut: 1998 vs Ireland

Honours: 54 England caps and 5 Lions caps

Magic moment: Dropping the winning goal in the 2003 World Cup Final

Did you know? When Jonny scored 27 points against Scotland in the 2007 Six Nations it was his first match for England in over three years because of injuries.

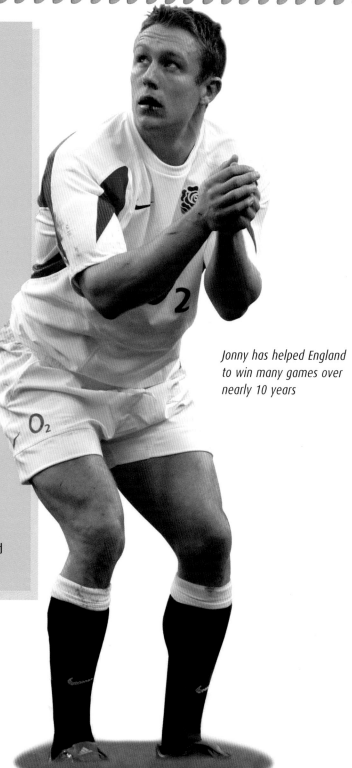

Jonny has helped England to win many games over nearly 10 years

Jonny has scored more Test points than any other English player. True or false?

Pass Master

Scoring tries, kicking goals, making tackles – these are the all-action moments on a rugby field, but what makes them all possible? That's right, being able to pass and catch the ball.

The first and most important thing to do is get used to the feel and shape of a rugby ball. A football or a cricket ball is easy to catch because it's round, but the oval shape of a rugby ball means you have to keep your eye on the ball at all times!

Hold the ball in two hands with your elbows slightly bent, just as Gavin Henson is doing in the photo. Notice how he's also about to swing his arms across his body as he makes the pass, and how he's looking at the player he's going to pass the ball to.

If you watch the great players like Gavin Henson on television you'll also notice that as they release the ball they flick it out of their hands using their wrist and fingers.

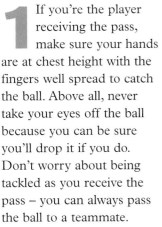

1 If you're the player receiving the pass, make sure your hands are at chest height with the fingers well spread to catch the ball. Above all, never take your eyes off the ball because you can be sure you'll drop it if you do. Don't worry about being tackled as you receive the pass – you can always pass the ball to a teammate.

2 A great way to practise your catching and passing is with your friends, but if they're busy, practise against a wall. The shape of the ball means it will bounce in all sorts of funny directions, so be on your toes because it could go anywhere!

Women on the Wing

If you thought rugby was just for men, think again! Women's rugby is one of the fastest growing sports in the world.

Women's rugby was first played in the 1970s and in 1983 the women's rugby union was formed in England, consisting of just 12 clubs. Now there are 410 clubs in the union, including more than 40 school sides. That's just in England alone; there are also women's clubs all around the world, from Scotland to Samoa, and from Canada to Australia.

But the best side in the world are New Zealand. They're called the 'Black Ferns' and just like the awesome New Zealand men's team, the 'Ferns' play in all black.

The Women's World Cup began in 1991 and the USA were the victors, beating England in the final. Four years later the English got their revenge, defeating America 38–23 to lift the cup. But the last three World Cups have all been won by New Zealand, with fly-half Anna Richards playing a starring role in each one.

In 1998 the Black Ferns beat the USA and in 2002 and 2006 it was England who finished runners-up. The 2006 final was a thriller, and it took a last-minute try by Ferns' full-back Amiria Marsh to clinch the World Cup for New Zealand.

The other major women's competition is the Six Nations. It began in 2001, although unlike the men's Six Nations there was a difference – Italy didn't have a team, but Spain did! However, Italy replaced Spain in 2007 so now the women's Six Nations is identical to the men's Six Nations – and it's just as exciting, featuring great players like England scrum-half Nolli Waterman and French captain Estelle Sartini.

England couldn't stop New Zealand winning the 2006 World Cup

The Dream Team

NO. **9**

Agustin Pichot

(Argentina)

Full name: Agustin Pichot

Position: Scrum-half

Born: 22 August 1974 in Buenos Aires, Argentina

Height: 175cm

Weight: 78kg

Club: Stade Français

Test debut: 1995 vs Australia

Honours: 58 caps for Argentina

Magic moment: Captaining Argentina to their first ever victory at Twickenham vs England in 2006

Did you know? Agustin scored Argentina's only try of the match in his debut in 1995

Which English club did Agustin captain?

Agustin Pichot inspired Argentina to victory over England in 2006

Terror Tackling

What makes rugby such a great and unique sport? It's not the tries or the scrums, it's the tackling. Making a tackle in football is easy, but in rugby it requires real courage.

People often think that only the big players can be terror tacklers, but that's nonsense! It's the timing that is most important – knowing the right moment to launch yourself at your opponent and stop him dead in his tracks! The bigger they are, the faster they fall!

Some of the smaller players in rugby – like England's Jonny Wilkinson or Ireland's Peter Stringer – are great tacklers because they time their tackles to perfection.

But whether you're a big tackler or a little tackler, what you must ALWAYS remember to do when you make a tackle is keep your head to one side. It's the golden rule of tackling.

Just look at the photo of England's Matthew Tait being tackled by South Africa's Wynand Olivier at Twickenham in 2006. What do you notice? That's right, Olivier makes sure his head isn't going to collide with Tait's legs.

On the next page you'll discover how to make the three types of tackle. Practise them with your friends, but start off slowly at walking pace, and then increase your speed until you feel really ready to tear into your tackles!

Matthew Tait is the victim of a good tackle by South Africa's Wynand Olivier

The tackle from behind

If your opponent is sprinting for the try line with no one to beat, the only way to stop him is with a tackle from behind.

1 Fix your eyes on the back of the ball-carrier's legs.

2 Wrap your arms around his legs, bring your shoulder against the back of his thighs and position your head to the side of his legs.

3 As you both fall, make sure you land on top of your opponent as this means you won't hit your shoulders on the ground.

The side-on tackle

Often you'll find yourself running across the pitch to make a tackle, sometimes using your left shoulder and other times your right.

1 As you near the ball-carrier pick a spot on his upper thighs and bend your torso.

2 Make contact with your shoulder and position your head BEHIND your opponent's legs.

3 Wrap your arms around his legs and use your weight and his momentum to bring him down with you landing on top of him.

The front-on tackle

This is the easiest tackle to make, even though it requires most bravery because the player is running straight at you!

1 Crouch in waiting as the ball-carrier approaches and decide which shoulder you are going to use to make the tackle.

2 Make contact with your shoulder, NOT your head – which should be positioned to one side of his legs – and encircle his thighs with your arms.

3 As you fall, use your weight and your opponent's momentum to twist round so you land of top of him.

And remember, after every tackle, jump to your feet and try to take the ball from the tackled player. But you MUST be on your feet when you go for the ball, otherwise it will be a penalty!

Sevens Heaven

Sevens rugby is now one of the most popular sports on the planet. It's part of the Commonwealth Games, there is a Sevens World Cup every four years and each season there is the Sevens World Series competition. Sevens is fast, it's furious and it's fun to watch. But it's all a long way from how Sevens rugby started.

Fiji in action against Portugal during the 2006 Dubai Sevens

It was way back in 1883 that a butcher in the small Scottish town of Melrose came up with the idea of seven-a-side rugby. Ned Haig wanted to raise money for Melrose rugby club, so he thought it would be a good idea to stage a tournament involving local teams. To make it more exciting for spectators, Haig reduced the teams from 15 to 7-a-side and each half lasted only seven minutes instead of the usual 40.

Sevens soon spread around the world and in 1926 the Middlesex Sevens started at Twickenham. They are still held today, as are the Melrose Sevens.

However, the most important Sevens tournaments today are the World Cup and the World Series. The first Sevens World Cup was held in 1993, and was won by England, but since then Fiji and New Zealand have dominated, with the Fijians lifting the cup in 2005.

The World Sevens Series is held each season and features eight competitions around the world, including in the USA, England and Hong Kong. New Zealand won the Series crown every year from 2000 to 2005, but Fiji triumphed in 2006.

As well as each half only lasting seven minutes, there are some other big differences in Sevens rugby compared to 15s. For instance, the half-time interval lasts only one minute; if a side scores a try the conversion must be drop-kicked and not kicked from a tee; and a scrum consists of just three players per team.

Seven Sevens Super Stats

1 **The final** of a Sevens tournament always lasts a little bit longer than the other matches. Instead of seven minutes each way, it's ten minutes and if it goes to extra-time the winner is the first side to score a try!

2 **One of** the most popular Sevens tournaments is the Rosslyn Park School Sevens, which is held each year in London. It began in 1939 and now involve over 7000 boys and girls between the ages of 13 and 19 from around the world.

3 **Although** the Hong Kong Sevens began in 1976 it wasn't until 2002 that England first won the competition, beating Fiji in the final.

4 **The trophy** awarded to the winning side in the Sevens World Cup is called the Melrose Cup, in honour of the town where Sevens was born.

5 **Sevens** was first played at the Commonwealth Games in 1998 and the gold medal was won by New Zealand. They also took first spot in 2002 and 2006.

6 **The greatest** ever Sevens player is Fijian Waisale Serevi, whose nickname is 'The Wizard'! He's not a big man, but has great pace and wonderful skills. The Wizard has won two World Cups, two Commonwealth silver medals and the 2006 World Series crown.

7 **One of** the most spectacular venues in the World Sevens Series is Dubai in the Middle East. In the 1990s the matches were played on sand but now there's a grass pitch, which means players no longer get sand in between their toes!

The Hong Kong Stadium is a magnificent setting for Sevens rugby

The Dream Team

NO. **8**

Simon Taylor

(Scotland)

Full name: Simon Marcus Taylor

Position: No 8

Born: 17 August 1979 in Stirling, Scotland

Height: 193cm

Weight: 114kg

Club: Edinburgh

Test debut: 2000 vs USA

Honours: 51 Scotland caps

Magic moment: Helping Scotland beat South Africa in 2002 for the first time in 33 years

Did you know? Simon toured Australia with the 2001 Lions but injured his knee and didn't play any Test matches

Scotland's Simon Taylor is a No 8 with power and pace

Try This!

Simon studied maths at university - true or false?

The European Cup

The European Cup began in 1995 when rugby became a professional sport. In the first year only 12 sides took part and it wasn't really a 'European' competition because English and Scottish clubs were too busy to get involved.

But twelve years later the European Cup has grown into the coolest club competition in the world. In the 2006 final 75,000 fans watched Irish side Munster beat French club Biarritz to win the cup, thanks to Ronan O'Gara who kicked 13 points. Not only has O'Gara got a European Cup winners' medal in his pocket, but the Irish fly-half has scored almost 1000 points in the competition – more than any other player!

Toulouse have won the cup three times

Martin Johnson shows off the European Cup in 2001

Although it was a mighty Munster performance to win the cup, they've still got some way to go before they beat Toulouse's record of three cup wins. The club from the south of France won the European Cup in 1996, 2003 and 2005. They also reached the final in 2004 but were beaten in a nail-biting match by London Wasps.

Only one team has ever lifted the European Cup in successive years and that was Leicester in 2001 and 2002, when England legend Martin Johnson captained them on both occasions.

The 2006–07 European Cup involved 24 teams from six different countries: England, Scotland, Ireland, Wales, France and Italy – and the final was played at Twickenham in front of a record 82,000 fans – proof that the competition just keeps getting bigger and better!

The Lions Roar

Every four years the best players from Britain and Ireland pull on the red jersey of the Lions.

Jerry Guscott drops a goal to help the Lions beat South Africa in 1997

Here's a stunning statistic to tell your friends! The British and Irish Lions played their first Test match in 1891 but in the following 116 years they've only played another 100 matches – 101 Tests in 116 years, that's not very many!

That's because the Lions are a unique team. Every four years the best players from England, Scotland, Ireland and Wales are selected to play three Test matches against either Australia, New Zealand or South Africa.

The most recent series of Test matches was against New Zealand in 2005, and the next will be against South Africa in 2009. Then, in 2013, the Lions will go 'Down Under' to take on Australia. Who knows, you might be one of them!

Because the Lions only play once every four years, it's a great honour to play for them. Some

of the world's best players have worn the famous jersey; legends like Martin Johnson of England, Scotland's Gregor Townsend, Brian O'Driscoll of Ireland and Rob Howley of Wales.

The first ever Lions tour was to Australia and New Zealand in 1888, although they didn't play any Test matches, but only games against local sides. In 1891 the Lions went to South Africa and won all three Test matches.

The Lions were very strong in the 1970s, when they won in New Zealand and South Africa, and in 1997 the Lions scored a famous series victory in South Africa, thanks to players such as Lawrence Dallaglio, Martin Johnson, Matt Dawson and Neil Jenkins.

Tour Tales

The first rugby tour took place in 1882 and the tradition is as strong as ever today.

Every year rugby teams tour different countries, not just playing matches but also learning a little about the culture of the place they're visiting.

In 2006, for example, **Scotland** toured **South Africa** and played two Test matches, but they also found time to visit local schools to help teach children how to play rugby.

The very first overseas rugby tour was way back in 1882, when a team from New South Wales in **Australia** travelled across the Tasman Sea to play some matches in **New Zealand**.

In 1888 a **British** side made its first tour, visiting **Australia** and **New Zealand.** The voyage by boat took six weeks, and the tourists played 35 matches between April and October.

That was nothing compared to the number of games played by a **New Zealand** side which arrived in **Britain** in August 1888. In the next seven months they played an amazing 74 matches, winning 49, losing 20 and drawing five. Sometimes they played four games a week – no wonder they were exhausted when they left!

The invention of the aeroplane made life much easier for rugby teams, and now rugby tours are shorter. The best two tours in recent years were made by **England** to **Australia** and **New Zealand** in 2003, when they beat both countries in great style, and by **New Zealand** to the British Isles in 2005. The **All Blacks** defeated **England**, **Ireland, Scotland** and **Wales** to achieve a '**Grand Slam**' tour!

Action from Scotland's tour to South Africa in 2006

Deadeye Drop Goal

Down the opposition with a drop goal.

Everyone remembers the 2003 World Cup Final between England and Australia! One minute of extra time remaining, the scores level at 17-17, and Jonny Wilkinson wins the cup for England with a glorious drop goal.

Like all great deadeye droppers, Jonny makes it look easy but dropping a goal takes a lot of practice and patience. If you follow the steps below it might not be long before you'll be sending the ball sailing between the posts!

1 Hold the ball in two hands at hip height and with your eyes looking at the ball, not the posts.

2 Drop (don't bounce) the ball to the ground as you bring your kicking foot back, ready to strike. Remember to keep watching the ball.

3 At the same time that the ball touches the ground, strike it with the front and inside of your foot.

4 Bring your kicking foot right through the line of the ball and only then raise your head to see where the ball is going.

Look at Jonny Wilkinson dropping the winning goal for England in the 2003 World Cup. Notice how he is watching the ball, how his kicking foot is drawn back ready to strike the ball and how his arms are spread wide to help him balance.

The Dream Team

Jerry's cousin is former All Black captain Tana Umaga – true or false?

NO. 7
Richie McCaw
(New Zealand)

Full name: Richard Hugh McCaw

Position: Flanker

Born: 31 December 1980 in Oamaru, New Zealand

Height: 188cm

Weight: 106kg

Club: Crusaders

Test debut: 2001 vs Ireland

Honours: 48 New Zealand caps

Magic moment: Captaining New Zealand to the 2006 Tri-Nations crown

Did you know? Richie was voted the World Player of the Year in 2006

NO. 6
Jerry Collins
(New Zealand)

Full name: Jerry Collins

Position: Flanker

Born: 4 November 1980 in Apia, Samoa

Height: 191cm

Weight: 107kg

Club: Hurricanes

Test debut: 2001 vs Argentina

Honours: 38 New Zealand caps

Magic moment: Captaining New Zealand for the first time vs Argentina in 2006

Did you know? Jerry didn't score his first try for New Zealand until his 20th match

Richie McCaw is one of the world's great players – in any position!

Is Richie an open-side or a blind-side flanker?

33

Rugby's Record Breakers

In rugby it's not just the rules that are sometimes broken!

Rugby is a great game for records – the most tries scored, the most games played, the most victories recorded. Here are some of rugby's remarkable record-breakers!

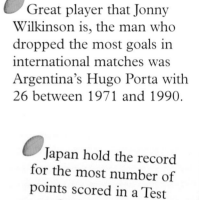

When it comes to scoring points, however, it's a Welshman who leads the way. Neil Jenkins scored 1049 points for Wales between 1991 and 2002. In addition, he also scored 41 points for the Lions in South Africa in 1997, giving a combined total of 1090.

Great player that Jonny Wilkinson is, the man who dropped the most goals in international matches was Argentina's Hugo Porta with 26 between 1971 and 1990.

At the start of 2007 Australian scrum-half George Gregan had won a record 127 caps since he made his debut in 1994. Second on the list of most-capped players is Englishman Jason Leonard with 114 appearances. What makes Leonard's so amazing is that he was a prop – the toughest position on the field!

Japan hold the record for the most number of points scored in a Test match. Against Chinese Taipei in 2002 they scored 155. That's nearly two points every minute of the game! How many points did poor Chinese Taipei score? Just three!

The player who holds the record for the most number of international tries is Japan's Daisuke Ohata. In 2006 he scored three tries against Georgia to overtake Australian David Campese's previous record of 64. By the end of 2006 Daisuke had scored 69 tries in 58 matches, and with the World Cup coming up, he's sure to add to that total.

George Gregan of Australia has won a record number of international caps

In 2003 Argentina nearly beat Japan's record when they walloped Paraguay 144–0, although they did create a record of their own in the match by scoring 24 tries. Not only that, but winger Jose Maria Nunez Piossek set his own record by scoring nine of the 24 tries.

And the record for the most number of consecutive defeats? That belongs to Scotland who between 1951 and 1955 lost 17 matches in a row. Now that's a record no country wishes to break!

Which is the best rugby side ever? Impossible to say, but two countries hold the record for the most number of consecutive victories. New Zealand won 17 matches in a row between 1965 and 1969, and so did South Africa, between 1997 and 1998.

Daisuke Ohata of Japan has scored more international tries than any other player

The biggest crowd at a rugby international was the 109,874 who crammed into the Telstra Stadium in Sydney in 2000 to see New Zealand win a thrilling match against Australia.

The Super 14

Fourteen fantastic teams fighting it out to be number one.

The Super 14 is the southern hemisphere's answer to the European Cup. Between February and May each year, fourteen teams from South Africa, Australia and New Zealand battle it out to see who is the hotshot of the south!

The competition began in 1996 with 12 teams, not 14. For the first two years New Zealand's Auckland Blues reigned supreme, thanks in no small part to their giant All Black wing, Jonah Lomu. In 1996 the Blues beat South Africa's Natal Sharks and the following year it was Australia's ACT Brumbies who finished runners-up. Since then, however, it's been another New Zealand side that has dominated. The Canterbury Crusaders have won a staggering six titles, including 2005 and 2006, and they've also finished runners-up twice.

The Crusaders' team boasts a host of All Blacks, including captain Richie McCaw, giant second-row Chris Jack and ace goal-kicker Daniel Carter. No wonder they're so wonderful!

The 2006 season was special for the competition because the number of teams increased from 12 to 14. For the first time, there were five teams from New Zealand, five from South Africa and four from Australia.

A South African side has never won the Super 14, although the Sharks have twice been runners-up, and the only Australian team to have triumphed is the Brumbies. They lifted the cup in 2001 and 2004 with a team that included Aussie legend George Gregan.

The Canterbury Crusaders have won a record number of Super 14 titles

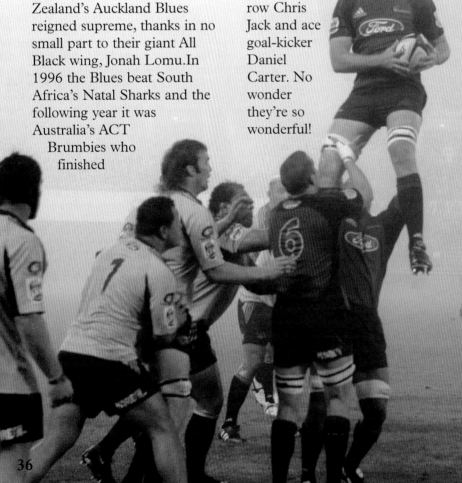

The Dream Team

NO. 4

Paul O'Connell
(Ireland)

Full name: Paul Jeremiah O'Connell

Position: Second row

Born: 20 October 1979 in Limerick, Ireland

Height: 198cm

Weight: 111kg

Club: Munster

Test debut: 2002 vs Wales

Honours: 42 Ireland caps and 3 Lions caps

Magic moment: Captaining Ireland to a record win vs Scotland in 2005

Did you know? Paul was a representative swimmer in his youth

NO. 5

Victor Matfield
(South Africa)

Full name: Victor Matfield

Position: Second row

Born: 11 May 1977 in Pietersburg, South Africa

Height: 200cm

Weight: 108kg

Club: Bulls

Test debut: 2001 vs Italy

Honours: 54 South Africa caps

Magic moment: Scoring the try that won South Africa the 2004 Tri-Nations title

Did you know? Victor is the captain of the Bulls

In which year did Paul and Munster win the European Cup?

At which other sport is Victor very good?

Any team would be happy to have Ireland's Paul O'Connell

Brilliant Backs and Fearsome Forwards

The backs get the chance to run with the ball so they need to be quick and skilful.

There are seven backs in a rugby team and you'll often hear them referred to as the 'back line'.

The Number 9 is called the scrum-half and he is the link between the forwards and the backs. The most important attribute for a scrum-half is his pass – it must be quick and accurate so that his team can attack the opposition. And a scrum-half must also have a loud voice because he needs to pass instructions between the forwards and the backs.

The fly-half wears Number 10 and he, more than any other player, controls the match. When the forwards win the ball, the scrum-half passes it to the fly-half and he must decide whether to kick, run or pass.

The two centres are numbers 12 and 13 and they operate in the 'centre' of the pitch. They must be quick and strong in attack, but also solid in defence and not afraid of tackling because teams often look to attack through centrefield.

Number 11 is the left winger and 14 is on the right wing. These two players are usually the fastest in the team because when they get the ball they're expected to scorch down the wing and score tries. In the olden days wingers were also the smallest players on the pitch, but nowadays wingers can be as big as flankers. Scary!

The full-back plays behind the other backs and is the last line of defence. Because of this he must be a good tackler – otherwise a try will be scored. In attack the full-back joins the back line with his fast and powerful running.

Who's your best back? Check out our Dream Team to see if he's in!

The forwards try to win possession for the backs so they need to be big and strong.

The flankers are called open-side and blind-side. The open-side flanker is smaller and quicker than the blind-side and must try to stop the opposition fly-half from controlling the game. The blind-side flanker also tackles a lot, but he concentrates more on disrupting the opposition forwards.

Who's your favourite forward? Delve into our Dream Team to see if he's been picked!

There are eight forwards in a rugby team, often referred to as the 'pack'. The front row consists of two props and a hooker. The props must be strong and heavy because they 'prop up' the scrum – in other words, they keep it steady. The hooker's job is to 'hook' back the ball when it is put into the scrum by the scrum-half, and he also throws the ball into the line-out.

The two second-rows are usually the tallest players in the team because their role is to jump in the line-out and win the ball. But they must also be strong because they need to push in the scrum.

The back-row consists of two flankers and a Number 8. All these players must be fit and skilful because they have many jobs to do. The Number 8 is often the tallest of the three and jumps in the line-out. He also picks the ball up from the scrum and attacks the opposition.

Running Rugby

If you want to be a real rugby star, you need to learn how to run with the ball.

You've taken a pass and now the ball is in your hands. What happens next? That's not as silly as it sounds! You're going to run with the ball and try to score a try, of course, but there's more to it than that.

When you run with the ball always hold it in two hands so it's about level with your belly button. That way it's much easier to pass the ball left or right if you see a teammate in support.

But what do you do if you see a big opponent approaching ready to tackle you and you've no teammate to pass to?

One option is to hand him off. To do this hold the ball in the arm furthest from the would-be tackler and with the free arm reach out and push away your opponent.

REMEMBER – the hand-off must be with the palm of your hand. If your hand is clenched, you'll be penalised for dangerous play and you might even be sent to the sin bin!

Another useful trick to avoid being tackled when you're running with the ball is the sidestep. As the tackler comes towards you, slow down slightly and decide whether you're going to go left or right. When you've decided, take a sudden big step away from the tackler with your outside leg.

Then, as you step away from the tackler, really push off with your inside leg. Don't forget to keep the ball in the arm furthest from the tackler just in case he makes a lunge for it.

The correct form of hand-off.

The incorrect form of hand-off.

The Dream Team

NO. 1

Carl Hayman
(New Zealand)

Full name: Carl Joseph Hayman

Position: Prop

Born: 14 November 1979 in Opunake, New Zealand

Height: 193cm

Weight: 115kg

Club: Highlanders

Test debut: 2001 vs Samoa

Honours: 35 New Zealand caps

Magic moment: When Carl made his debut in 2001 he became the 1000th player to wear the All Black shirt

Did you know? Carl first pulled on a black jersey when he played for New Zealand Under-16s in 1995

NO. 3

Phil Vickery
(England)

Full name: Philip John Vickery

Position: Prop

Born: 14 March 1976 in Barnstaple, Devon

Height: 190cm

Weight: 121kg

Club: London Wasps

Test debut: 1998 vs Wales

Honours: 52 England caps and 3 Lions caps

Magic moment: Winning the 2003 World Cup

Did you know? Big Phil played in all seven England games in the 2003 World Cup tournament

Carl played for New Zealand Maori against the Lions in 2005 – true of false?

What happened to Phil in January 2007?

England captain Phil Vickery is also a superb prop

On Top of the World

Only twenty years after the Rugby World Cup began, it has become the third biggest global sports event after the soccer World Cup and the Olympics.

It took rugby a long time to organise a World Cup but the first tournament in 1987 proved to be an instant success. Sixteen countries took part and in the final New Zealand beat France 29–9 with 600 million people around the world watching the match on television.

Four years later the World Cup was held in Britain and France, but it was a team from the southern hemisphere, Australia, who triumphed in the final, defeating England 12–6.

In 1995 the tournament was hosted by South Africa and it was during this World Cup that a new star was born. His name was Jonah Lomu and he played for New Zealand on the wing – even though he was big enough to be a second row! The giant Jonah scored seven tries in the tournament, including four against England in the semifinal, but it wasn't enough to help New Zealand lift the cup. They lost to South Africa 15–12 in the final.

Four years later Australia won the cup (named the Webb Ellis trophy in honour of the boy who invented rugby in 1823) for a second time when they beat France in the final in Cardiff. The Aussies had a chance of making it a fabulous three World Cup victories in 2003, but in a thrilling match they were beaten 20–17 by England, thanks to a drop goal from Jonny Wilkinson in the last minute of the match!

The 2007 World Cup starts in September in France with 20 countries taking part from around the world. As well as the likes of New Zealand and England, there'll also be teams from as far away as Canada, Fiji and Japan. But no matter how far they've travelled to get to France, all 20 teams will have only one thing on their minds – getting their hands on the little gold cup.

Jonah Lomu scores against England in the 1995 World Cup

New Zealand's Jonah Lomu scored 15 World Cup tries in the 1995 and 1999 tournaments – a record that is sure to stand for many years to come.

Scotsman Gavin Hastings has scored more World Cup points than anyone else. His total of 227 is 32 more than second place Michael Lynagh of Australia.

Not surprisingly, Jonny Wilkinson of England holds the record for the greatest number of dropped goals in World Cup matches with eight – and they were all scored in the 2003 tournament!

It's another Englishman, Jason Leonard, who has the record for the most number of World Cup appearances. The big prop played in 22 matches between his first game in 1991 and his last in 2003. His old teammate, Martin Johnson, is second with 18.

The most number of points scored by a team in a World Cup match is the 145 New Zealand ran up against Japan in 1995.

That match also saw another record – most points scored by one player in a game. Simon Culhane of New Zealand kicked 45, one more than the 44 scored by Gavin

Hastings against the Ivory Coast in the same year.

Although Jonny Wilkinson holds the record for the most number of World Cup dropped goals, the highest number of goals dropped in a single match were the five landed by South Africa's Jannie de Beer against England in 1999.

New Zealand have won more World Cup matches than any other team with 26 victories and only five defeats. Unfortunately for the men in black three of those defeats came in semi-finals and another in a final.

England's Martin Johnson played in 18 World Cup matches

The Calcutta Cup

Why do England and Scotland compete for a cup named after an Indian city?

1 England and Scotland played each other in the first ever rugby international in 1871 and although the Scots won they didn't receive a trophy. But from 1879 onwards a cup has been presented to the winning side, thanks to a small rugby club on the other side of the world!

2 The Calcutta rugby club was formed in 1873 by British people living and working in India. At first the club was a great success, but gradually the very hot weather in India made the game less popular as people preferred tennis and croquet and other less energetic sports.

3 So in 1878 the Calcutta club was closed down and the last of the club's coins were used to make a silver cup. It was called the Calcutta Cup and it was presented to the English rugby union as a prize for the annual match against Scotland.

4 As you can see in the photo it's a beautiful cup with its handles made to look like snakes, and an elephant on top – that's because both these animals are found around Calcutta! The city is now called Kolkata but the trophy remains the Calcutta Cup.

5 Although the cup was first played for in 1879, that match ended in a draw and it wasn't until 1880 that a team lifted the Calcutta Cup in triumph, when England beat Scotland.

6 The 114th Calcutta Cup match was played at Twickenham in 2007 when England had an overwhelming victory, winning 42–20. Although England have won more matches than Scotland, the Scots have had some great victories.

7 Perhaps the most famous was in 1990 in the famous 'Grand Slam' decider. It was the last match of that season's Five Nations and whoever won would claim the Grand Slam. England were the favourites but Scotland pulled off a fantastic 13–7 win.

Martin Corry lifts the Calcutta Cup following England's win in 2005

44

Count the Cups

There are more cups and trophies to be won in rugby than ever before.

For many years the Calcutta Cup was the only major trophy awarded in international rugby – but only two countries could ever win it. That was hardly very fair!

Things began to change in 1987 when the World Cup began and the Webb Ellis Trophy was awarded to the world champions. Now there are lots of other cups up for grabs in international rugby.

Since 1997 England and Australia have contested the Cook Cup – named after the famous explorer Captain Cook – and the current holders are Australia.

Australia also play South Africa each year for the Nelson Mandela Challenge Plate – in honour of former South African president Nelson Mandela – and Australia are the reigning champs!

The Churchill Cup is named after Winston Churchill, Britain's famous prime minister, and is contested each year by Canada, USA and England.

In 1988 England and Ireland began competing for the Millennium Trophy and in the last few years the Irish have dominated, winning in 2004, 2005 and 2006.

Ireland also play Australia for the Lansdowne Cup (it takes its name from Ireland's home ground of Lansdowne Road) and in 2006 the Irish beat Australia to lift the cup.

However, the most famous trophy in rugby – apart from the Calcutta Cup and the World Cup – is the Bledisloe Cup, which is contested between Australia and New Zealand. The cup is named after Lord Bledisloe, who was Governer-General of New Zealand, and he donated it in 1931.

New Zealand have lifted the Bledisloe Cup more times than Australia, but whenever the cup is at stake you can be sure both sides are desperate to get their hands on the biggest cup in antipodean rugby!

New Zealand celebrate winning the 2006 Bledisloe Cup

The Magic Touch

Being able to kick the ball a long way into touch is a useful skill to have for any kicker.

The kick to touch, or 'punt' as it's often called, can help your team in both attack and defence. Imagine if your side has been awarded a penalty close to your own try-line. What better way to ease the pressure on your team than by kicking the ball into touch on the halfway line? Your teammates will give you a big pat on the back!

Then if you're awarded another penalty close to the halfway line, you can punt the ball into touch close to their opposition try-line. Suddenly, instead of your team being under pressure, it's your opponents who are getting nervous – all because of two top touch-finding kicks!

So here's how to do it.

1 Hold the ball at waist level so that it is angled away from your body. If you're right-handed have the left hand at the front of the ball and the right hand further back (vice-versa for left-handers).

2 Step forward and drop the ball on to your foot, while making sure your eyes are on the ball and not looking at where you want it to land.

3 The ball should make contact with the part of your boot between the toe and the laces. Keep the foot pointed towards the ground as you strike the ball and follow through so the foot ends up at waist height.

You can practise your punting by kicking a ball to a friend. First start by standing ten metres apart, then move back as you become more confident until you're fifty metres apart. But remember to mind those windows!

46

The Dream Team

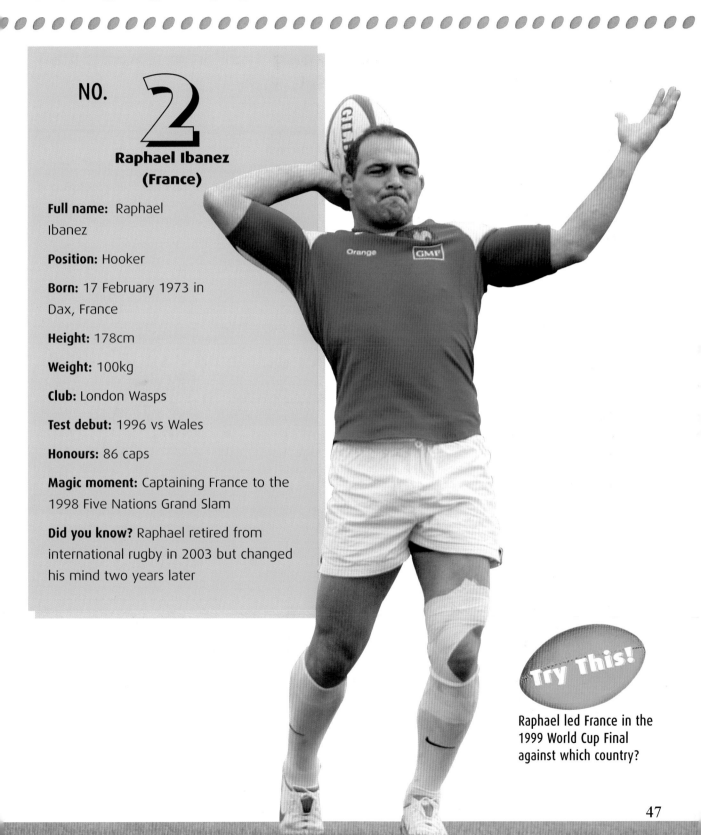

NO. 2

Raphael Ibanez
(France)

Full name: Raphael Ibanez

Position: Hooker

Born: 17 February 1973 in Dax, France

Height: 178cm

Weight: 100kg

Club: London Wasps

Test debut: 1996 vs Wales

Honours: 86 caps

Magic moment: Captaining France to the 1998 Five Nations Grand Slam

Did you know? Raphael retired from international rugby in 2003 but changed his mind two years later

Try This!

Raphael led France in the 1999 World Cup Final against which country?

The Great Games

Rugby matches are always full of thrills and spills but these four games were simply stupendous!

Scotland beat England 13–7 in 1990 in the last match of the Five Nations championship. England had scored a brilliant try in the first half but in the second half Tony Stanger touched down for the Scots to give his side the Grand Slam – only the third in their history!

France staged a magical comeback against New Zealand in 1999 when the two sides met in the semi-final of the World Cup. Jonah Lomu smashed his way over the French try-line twice to give his side a comfortable lead, but France scored three second-half tries to win 43–31. Formidable!

Over 100,000 fans in **Sydney** saw an epic match between Australia and New Zealand in 2000. In the first few minutes the All Blacks scored 24 points but at half-time the Aussies had drawn level. Then in the second half they took the lead, but with just seconds left, Jonah Lomu scored the try that won the game for New Zealand 39–35.

Wales won their first Grand Slam for 27 years in 2005 and even though they played brilliant rugby in all their matches, the win against France in Paris was awesome. France led 15–6 at half-time, but Wales came out firing after the break and scored two tries to clinch a 24–18 victory.

Answers to **TRY THIS**
p5 Wing; p8 centre; Jonah Lomu; p11 yellow; p14 His initials; Charlotte Church; p20 True; p23 Bristol; p28 False, it was law; p33 True; Open-side; p37 2006; Cricket; p41 True; He was appointed England captain; p47 Australia

PHOTO CREDITS

All photographs are © Getty Images, except where stated.
Cover images:
Josh Lewsey by Phil Cole
All Blacks by Jacques Demarthon, AFP
Chris Paterson by David Rogers
Brian O'Driscoll by Chris McGrath
P1/P32 Jonny Wilkinson by Damien Meyer, AFP
P2/P23 Richie McCaw by Richard Heathcote, AFP
P4 Hilton Lobberts by AFP
P5 Josh Lewsey by David Rogers
P8/back cover flap Lote Tuqiri by Stu Forster
P9 Webb Ellis Trophy by Pascal Guyot, AFP
P10 Francois Pienaar by David Rogers
P12 Ronan O'Gara by Warren Little
P14 Brian O'Driscoll by Paul Kane
P15 The Pacific Islanders by Glenn Campbell, AFP
P18 Welsh team by Getty Images
P19 France v Wales by AFP
P20 Jonny Wilkinson by Shaun Botterill
P21/cover Gavin Henson by David Rogers
P22 England v New Zealand by Tim Smith
P23 Agustin Pichot by Damien Meyer, AFP
P24 Matthew Tait & Wynand Olivier by Odd Andersen, AFP
P26 Fiji v Portugal by Karim Sahib, AFP
P27 Hong Kong Stadium by Chris McGrath
P28 Simon Taylor by Martin Hayhow, AFP
P29 Martin Johnson by David Rogers
P29 Toulouse team by Richard Heathcote
P30 Jeremy Guscott by Getty Images
P31 Scotland team by AFP
P33/front cover Richie McCaw by Richard Heathcote, AFP
P34 George Gregan by Chris McGrath
P35 Daisuke Ohata by Toshifumi Kitamura, AFP
P36 The Canterbury Crusaders by Ross Land
P37 Paul O'Connell by Sandra Mu
P41 Phil Vickery by David Rogers
P42 Jonah Lomu by Simon Bruty
P43 Martin Johnson by Chris McGrath
P44 Martin Corry by Richard Heathcote
P45 New Zealand team by Jeff Brass
P47 Raphael Ibanez by Damien Meyer, AFP
P48 Martyn Williams by Damien Meyer, AFP

Martyn Williams scores for Wales against France in 2005